Mr. Tenkey's

100 TIPS

TO WIN IN THE MORTGAGE INDUSTRY

Ignore At Your Peril...

Christopher M. Mason

ISBN: 978-1-54397-883-4 (print)
ISBN: 978-1-54397-884-1 (ebook)

FOREWORD

When I first read a draft of this book, I thought the author had been reading my mind the last 30 years. He and I have had many discussions over the years, and we share the same views about what it takes to be successful in mortgage banking. What a gift to the industry that he chose to put his views down on paper.

His opening line talks about an industry driven by salesmanship and personality, characteristics whose value has diminished dramatically. What I've seen over the years is that what was once a high margin business has evolved into one where every basis point matters, and there is no room for error. Having a charismatic leader is no longer enough. Not even close.

When I started in the industry in 1977, mortgage banking was an obscure business with few competitors and wide margins. The banks pretty much owned the conventional market, and mortgage bankers dominated FHA and VA lending. Mortgage companies didn't compete with the banks for conventional business, and the banks left the mortgage companies alone to do the government loans. It was a small sandbox, and there just weren't that many mortgage companies playing in it.

So all in all, it was a high profit business. Extraordinarily high profit. Successful mortgage companies were usually led by people with charismatic personalities, and rah-rah salesmanship was an all-important ingredient. With margins so high, companies could also be sloppy.

Things have changed. The single-family mortgage has been commoditized. Mortgage banking is no longer about charisma, personality, and salesmanship. They may still have a role to play, but that role is minuscule compared with what matters in any commodity business.

I'll let the readers see for themselves what really matters. And the best part of this book is that the author's suggestions are all very practical.

This book may challenge the way you think about the mortgage business. And by the time you finish it, you just might have found the keys to surviving and thriving.

Joe Garrett
Garrett, McAuley & Co.
www.GarrettMcauley.com

PREFACE

Hereafter lies the blood, sweat and tears of my years…in an industry that promotes itself on salesmanship and ego…

And what does a lone numbers guy do?

Well join them, of course! Create a new version of myself…and hopefully help others along the way.

And that doesn't mean just providing tips and advice to leadership, but hopefully providing a voice to the unsung heroes of the back office…whose work often gets overshadowed or ignored.

Well NO LONGER! I have found my voice, and I'm gonna use it. Use it to promote the work ethic I learned from my Grandpa, working vacations and summers, in his convenience store…where he would make me stock the shelves and then come by and re-check my work. If it wasn't up to standard, he would push all the cans I just worked on to the back of the shelf and tell me to "start over!" Needless to say, I wasn't happy…but I did learn that if I was gonna do something, do it once and do it right.

Use it to promote the ingenuity I learned from my Dad. He taught me the skills to take on any task and fake it until you make it…and in the process find out that most others are doing the same thing. Tasks are just that; don't be scared to try anything and go for it.

Use it to promote the drive and money management I learned from my Mom. She often said (which I still repeat to this day), "If you don't have the cash, you can't afford it." It's like she knew I was gonna be an accountant from day one.

So, I hope you enjoy the journey through my tips and concepts…and that it sparks forward movement in your own thoughts and ideas.

But before I let you go, a special shout out to Joe Garrett, for his sparking of my literary endeavor…

And a very special thank you to my partner, Justin Wassinger, for his listening of all my crazy book banter and his continued encouragement through it all.

Enjoy the read.

Christopher M. Mason

#1

Dear Management,

To those of you who base loan officer (LO) performance off units...

Please stop.

Remember, "Units drive cost, volume drives profit."

Yours Truly,

Mr. Tenkey

#2

Dear Management,

Do you know what your daily unit average (per funding day) is, for such items as:

1. Leads

2. Triggered apps

3. Submitted to processing, underwriting (U/W)

4. Fundings

You should…

If done right, it can tell you where you've been and where you're going.

Yours Truly,

Mr. Tenkey

#3

Dear Management,

Do you know the minimum loan volume that each loan officer should meet to earn their keep?

You should...

If done right, it will tell you which loan officers are pulling their weight, and more importantly, those who are not.

Yours Truly,

Mr. Tenkey

#4

Dear Management,

OK, so you have the minimum loan level for an LO figured out.

Now what?

You should...

Ask yourself a few questions on that lower tier. Do you need to train them more? Do you move them to outside sales? Or do you let them go?

After that, go out and thank all the other LOs who are carrying the burden of those unproductive LOs you currently have on the books.

Yours Truly,

Mr. Jenkey

#5

Dear Management,

OK, so quickly rank the top loan officers you have.

Are you sure you're right?

If you haven't compared their product mix, against the costs they generate…then you're most likely gonna be very surprised by the results.

Yours Truly,

Mr. Tenkey

#6

Dear Management,

Remember my tiny little rant of "volume drives profit, not units"?

Well to continue that rant...but not all volume drives profit, well at least not worthy of a reward.

Easy example: Think Jumbo (great volume, terrible margin)...but there are lots of other hidden landmines within the various product realms...

Be diligent, people.

Yours Truly,

Mr. Jenkey

#7

Dear Management,

Be very wary of an outside party who claims they can create all the cohesion in your company you've ever wanted!

Your company's culture is not a commodity... A commodity can be bought, culture CANNOT.

Culture can only be created and/or sustained by:

1. Ownership that demonstrates the culture by their own actions.

2. Management that hires, trains, and fires based on those actions.

3. Employees who accept/agree with the honesty of both 1 and 2.

So why do I (a simple numbers guy) care?

Because A LOT of money is being spent trying to create something, that otherwise can be found in a $5 mirror...

Yours Truly,

Mr. Tenkey

#8

Dear Management,

Have you always had an issue with the way those dang accountants handle booking income on mandatory loans?

You know, the way it throws off your margins month to month?

Well, if you can get them to separate out the pair-off activity from the pipeline activity, and follow a 90-day view, you'll have a much better predictive base for better forecasting and budgeting models.

Yours Truly,

Mr. Jenkey

#9

Dear Management,

Where do you feel the pendulum lands when judging the importance of the Sales versus Ops/Admin sides of your company?

The answer should be, "dead center between the two." The best companies are those that understand the importance of both sides of the company.

And that respect for both, then shines through to the whole company.

If a company has a weak sales force, the company starves from lack of production and momentum.

But if the company has a weak Ops/Admin force, the company starves from a lack of referrals and customer disapproval, buybacks, etc.

Yours Truly,

Mr. Tenkey

#10

Dear Management,

Do you know what the break-even point is for every profit center in your organization?

If the answer is no, you should.

Otherwise you could be punishing the whole organization for the sins of a few.

Yours Truly,

Mr. Jenkey

#11

Dear Management,

Do you think pull-thru is JUST how many leads you receive, as compared to how many loans you fund?

Well if you do, you're missing KEY METRICS to finding strengths and weaknesses in your company's origination process.

Yours Truly,

Mr. Tenkey

#12

Dear Management,

Be cautious of promoting a "We are family!" work environment…

Now, before you start, I'm not saying friendship, respect, and loyalty cannot occur or be earned through the employment process.

But the best companies I've seen run their organizations like a championship team. A team that recruits the best players…with the best skill sets…to win the game at hand.

Because decisions are needed, and some require teammates to be benched or kicked off the team…or a third-string player put in to replace a first-string team-mate who is no longer performing.

Holding on too strongly to a "family" mindset can stop you from making the hard decisions needed to run a great and efficient organization.

Yours Truly,

Mr. Tenkey

#13

Dear Management,

Evaluating a new Loan Officer or Branch to bring on…but getting sticker shock by the signing bonuses that still persist out there…

Well, are you thinking outside the box? How about an idea of paying them "?" bps (basis points) for 3, 6, or 9 months, which (based on THEIR OWN volume projections) would give them more money than a bonus?

The company would at least have the production, instead of the many cases I've seen…where the LO/Branch ends up underperforming and leaving or even worse, lingers on…draining resources…

And a question: If they do hesitate at this kind of proposal, think…the LO/Branch doth protest too much???

Yours Truly,

Mr. Tenkey

#14

Dear Management,

Copier leases...the bane of my existence, but a necessity until the day we can truly go paperless...[laughing as I type that part].

Side note: I just learned how to print directly to a pdf and not have to print and then scan. It's TRANSFORMATIONAL people!

Anyway, a couple tips here. Make sure the leases are contiguous through a master lease...gives you much more negotiation power...one end date versus multiple.

Also, while "buying" a copier and just getting a service contract sounds great, generally the numbers don't pencil out with growing companies needing flexibility.

Yours Truly,

Mr. Jenkey

#15

Dear Management,

Has "LO task creep" set in?

You know, that thing that starts out innocent...creating teams of people to support the sales staff from doing admin tasks…so they can focus on "selling"?

Company prospers! Yeah! Winning!

But then reality hits...markets go the other direction, and you see the inefficient monster that production hid.

But you know what? It can be repaired…and requiring an LO to submit/work up a strong, complete file to processing IS NOT a bad thing.

Neither is centralized or regionalized processing, admin staff, marketing assistants, LOAs, etc., or some hybrid of it all...

COMPETITION is on the march, people...in the form of automation, artificial intelligence, margin compression, banks and credit unions (CUs) strong in the market again, etc.

Changes in thinking ARE needed. Is your team up for the challenge?

Yours Truly,

Mr. Tenkey

#16

Dear Management,

Do you get a daily report of your total open pipeline?

Is it broken out by branch, LO, product characteristic (loan type, lien, channel, FICO, etc.)?

Do you know how much is triggered? Locked? Or what stage of operation the loan is in?

All these questions should be answered with…"Yes, and we also look at…"

Yours Truly,

Mr. Tenkey

#17

Dear Management,

Are you following the latest trend in business modeling...you know..."Hope"?

I think the formal naming convention is the "Hope and a Prayer" model.

Forget that... no matter what stage in a company's life-cycle you are, THINK FORWARD, people. Where do you want your company to go? What do you want your company to be when you get there?

Once that is set, you'll know what operations level, and which production/marketing strategies and technological innovations, you'll need to hit that goal.

Yours Truly,

Mr. Tenkey

#18

Dear Management,

Do you know what the life-cycle of your loans are (now I'm talking generally here) from Lead to Funded?

You should…but for this tip, let's say its 3 months.

So knowing that and (based on an earlier tip), knowing the loan types of those loans coming down the pipeline…

You are now able to get a 1- to 2-month heads-up on where your margins are going and proactively react.

That's a good thing, people…

Yours Truly,

Mr. Jenkey

#19

Dear Management,

What do you know about your "limbo" loans...you know, those loans funded but not yet sold? Also known as LHFS (loans held for sale) by some...

Do you know how long they are held on your warehouse lines? How long secondary is taking to register them? How long shipping is taking to get them moved? How long your investors are taking to purchase them? Which investors push back with the most "stips"? Among other things...

You should...

You should also have a good idea of the cash generated from each purchase, and be using that in your cash-flow management.

Yours Truly,

Mr. Tenkey

#20

Dear Management,

How many of you have the head of compliance in your operational planning/forecasting meetings?

You should…

Of course, that's if you've chosen the right person. Just like with us accountants, you don't want someone who fits the stereotype (snore fest…).

But let's say you've chosen correctly…a good compliance person will help give you advice you don't want to hear, help you navigate the "compliance overload" we are living in, and give you strong recommendations for your "should do's" and "must do's."

By including them in the process, you will create the MOST EFFICIENT way to get loans through the system…in the MOST COMPLIANT way.

Yours Truly,

Mr. Tenkey

#21

Dear Management,

So how good are you at estimating your month-end production numbers...for the following month 1, 2, or 3?

The answer should be within a tolerance of less than 5% for the first month and a little more lenient in months 2 and 3.

Those who say they know beyond that, usually have a bridge to sell ya too...

To get there, you'll need a good handle on expected closing dates, pull-thru rates, status trending, understanding market demands, etc.

Start with historical numbers and practice your models with the results you already have.

Good luck.

Yours Truly,

Mr. Tenkey

#22

Dear Management,

Let's talk about black holes. You know, that place in space where nothing comes out, not even light…or did I mean to say the IT department?

Now, now…IT can be a tool of greatness, OR it can be left to explore the great frontier, boldly going where no one has gone before… along with LOTS of money and resources…

So…small/mid-sized companies, be careful. At your size, you're not going to be leading edge…nor are you going to have "start from scratch" ideas. Focus on your strengths; don't get distracted by shiny new things. Choose well, stay in the lane of tested technology, push the benefits of your size, push the tried and true sales tactic that will never leave mortgage lending…the human factor.

Larger companies, be careful too. Heed my warnings above…they apply to you, too. Size doesn't protect you from making dumb decisions and losing lots of money…why do that? In-house technology can be your way to outmaneuver your competition. But again, think wisely and make sure the "new" way is efficient, the best process, and outperforms what can be bought off the shelf. It needs to warrant the cost and MOST IMPORTANTLY provide a healthy ROI that is worth the exploration…

Yours Truly,

Mr. Tenkey

#23

Dear Management,

How many commission pay structures/formats do you have?

If it's more than one...WHY?

What if I told you I could give you ONE structure that could fit any loan officer, with any production level, for any region or any product mix—with no need for commission caps—and that includes pricing exceptions/tolerance cures in the mix too?

Got your attention now?

Well, I can't give away all my secrets (maybe if I write another book). But believe me, it can be done. (Hint: Once you know how much a loan officer brings to the table, you're halfway there.)

Never stop being creative, people. And more importantly...never stop looking for a simpler method of doing everything.

Yours Truly,

Mr. Tenkey

#24

Dear Management,

Do you keep a daily/dynamic cash flow forecast?

Now, I'm not talking about the "all the worlds align" forecast that you create for prospective investors...I'm talking a down-and-dirty forecast that shows, 3 months out, where your balance lands daily?

You should...

It needs to include estimates of your weekly A/P, pairoff amounts, cash from funded loans, rent payments, large monthly payments, out-of-the-ordinary things, etc., and of course payroll. And don't forget those WH (warehouse) covenant minimums you need to stay above.

Because I don't care if you have money at the end of this process, I only care if you'll have the money you need 3 weeks from Thursday, or 5 weeks from Monday.

FYI: Employees don't like to be handed IOUs for their paychecks...that would be very NOT good, people!

Yours Truly,

Mr. Jenkey

#25

Dear Management,

Do you maintain a listing of EPOs (early pay off), EPDs (early payment default), indemnities, etc., and review it regularly?

You should...

It's always good to keep an eye on several things that this report can show you. Is there a pattern with certain investors? Is there a pattern with a certain LO or branch? Is there a pattern with a geographical area? Is there a pattern with market conditions, or even worse, a negative pattern in your own loan quality?

Now, not all is lost...in the mitigation arena, depending on the wording of your comp agreements, there may be some partial recovery...in the commissions paid to the LO. Every bit counts these days.

Stay diligent, people. Income leakage from these types of losses can have dramatic, and often hidden consequences, until it's too late...

Yours Truly,

Mr. Tenkey

#26

Dear Management,

Do you have a listing of your production, broken out by loan program?

Now I'm talking beyond how much conventional, government, and jumbo you may have. Dive deep... have details of all the specific loan adjustment factors, credit scores, locations, etc...

And take a look at those loan types you spent hours and hours setting up...you know, the ones the LOs said they JUST HAD TO HAVE to compete...and now, a year later, you've done one loan?

Let this reporting tell you where to focus, and more importantly where NOT to focus. Listen to what the market is saying, and see if your reporting is telling the same story.

You have a pot of gold in your own data. Go mine it, people!

Yours Truly,

Mr. Tenkey

#27

Dear Management,

In Tip 26, I mentioned having a listing of loan products funded. Let's continue that line of thought.

Do you also have a listing of production, broken out by who you sold it to?

Why? Because maintaining too many investors is VERY inefficient...but maintaining too few can be a bad thing too.

Pressure points of this area, as I see them:

1. Make sure you ALWAYS have at least two investors on tap to sell each and every product offering you have. Three investor options are even better. You NEVER want to be holding an unsalable loan. Not good, people...

2. Now I mentioned three investor options above...but for smaller shops this might be difficult with lower production niche loans. Investors are cutting companies off if they don't see the volume flow. And I can understand, they need to make money too... But NEVER go below two. Not worth the risk, in my eyes.

3. And speaking of eyes, always keep an eye on maintenance. Too many unused investors take up valuable time in maintenance of renewals, and updates of product compliance and overlays being disseminated throughout your systems. And for what? Busy work for your back office, to close that one very special investor's loan every 2 years?

Be diligent, peeps!

Yours Truly,

Mr. Tenkey

#28

Dear Management,

Do you maintain a breakout of office leases? And I'm not talking equipment leases again, but rather the actual space your butt sits...

Why? Because it's one of the largest expenses on the books. It demands attention.

Does your list include EVERY space, nook, and cranny you lease? Does it list the tiers of costs over the life of the lease? Or include the profit centers? Or the CAMs (common area maintenance)? Or special instructions on cash-outs, renewal notice dates, etc.? Or if it's a sub-lease? Or the square footage? Or (add important characteristic here)...

It should...yep, every single question/warning you need to make a decision about what is the cost? Should we renew? When do we notify the landlord for "x"? Who is using the space?

Is there capacity for more staff? Should we close this office?

Be diligent, peeps!

Yours Truly,

Mr. Tenkey

#29

Dear Management,

In these tough times, one thing does get easier...it's taking off the rose-colored glasses.

So in that vein, can we all take a deep breath and—all together now—"Just because an LO can "top produce," doesn't mean they can "top manage."

Managing people and/or expenses, recruiting, training, etc. are all very different skillsets from those of being a great salesperson. Finding people with all those in one deck of cards is a special gift indeed...

So don't get trapped into giving job titles as rewards for production skills...give them based on proven skillsets.

Let your bottom line see the rewards instead...

Yours Truly,

Mr. Tenkey

#30

Dear Management,

Lots of moving parts...with branches coming in and branches going out... these days.

So don't forgot to keep all those licenses up to date... because the regulators and your investors won't.

Remember to add and subtract branch locations at the state and local levels, FHA and others, insurance and bonding, etc. It can stop fundings in their tracks or get ya into trouble with the men in black...or is it gray or blue? Anyone know what the regulators wear these days?

Anyway, be diligent, peeps!

Yours Truly,

Mr. Tenkey

#31

Dear Management,

What is the number one rule in marketing???

Know your audience...and know THEIR preferences/needs, NOT yours.

Say you like paper surveys at the closing table...but research says your borrowers like online surveys...guess what you should do? NOT what you like.

Say you want the website to look like a, b, and c...but research says different features like x, y, and z drive more interest...guess what you should do? NOT what you want.

Define your customer...research THEIR wants and needs, remove your bias, have a highly COST-effective marketing campaign, and SELL LOANS.

Otherwise, yet another black hole of time and money...

Yours Truly,

Mr. Tenkey

#32

Dear Management,

How long does it take for you to make a substantial decision? Do you change that decision shortly after? Multiple times?

The wrong answer to these questions can really be detrimental...in terms of LOTS of wasted time/efforts and more importantly, MONEY!

If it takes you more than the length of a meeting, involving your key people...something is awry (remember, these are the people you hired to give you sound advice).

I'll leave it to you to figure out what the fix is (hint: it may not be them).

And if you change your mind after a vetted decision is made...for a NOT fully vetted reason?

UGH, the inefficiency...the mis-communication...the stifling effect on future decisions...the loss of a free-flow of ideas...the lack of luster on your leadership.

I'll leave it up to you to figure out what I think of that one (hint: not good, people).

Yours Truly,

Mr. Jenkey

#33

Dear Management,

So...like many companies...you have a Director of First Impressions at your front desk to welcome new borrowers and make them feel special. Do you use that same thought process in designing your HR department?

You should...

It is a far more critical function...this is a service industry...your best asset is your people. Why would you have the person handling "all that is important to them" NOT be in the forefront and sitting at the big-persons' table?

Just as important as having a financial voice, an operations voice, a tech voice, a compliance voice, a sales voice...a voice for your employees is JUST as important.

Repeat after me: "Treat your employees the best, and they'll take care of the rest!"

Because at the end of the day, a wage is a wage is a wage...and there is always another place down the street to find that.

But a great working environment, respect, and engagement...will win the day AND the employee's loyalty every time.

Yours Truly,

Mr. Tenkey

#34

Dear Management,

Trending projections continue to NOT be great for margins and production... something has to give...

And you can only cut operations so far...and you can only shrink leases so quickly... and you can only break even or tap into the coffers for so long...

So what's left?

The sacred cow...LO comp...bum bum bummmmm...

Competition for the almighty VOLUME has raised commissions to an unsustainable level. The pie can only be divided so many ways...their piece can't keep getting bigger...and the rest of us don't want less pie...

Something has to give. A change is coming. You know it, and they DO know it. Who will blink first??? But once one company pushes that domino completely, ooohhh, the waterfall that will occur.

Be smart until then. Start with the lower producers first. I mean, the amounts that have been paid for this level of production...sheesh (break even after like 2+ years...WHAT?).

Then go after the unproductive, and operations time suckers...this may even be a top producer...

Remember, just because there is LOTS of volume doesn't mean they make you lots of dollars.

NET MARGIN is the name of the game. LIVE THERE!

Yours Truly,

Mr. Jenkey

#35

Dear Management,

In a meeting once: "How will we know how much margin we have to play with if we go after a new location? They're not gonna tell us or even know what their margin is."

I took a deep breath and did my best Van Wilder... "Au contraire, mon frères... yes...yes...there is a way to find this out."

First, who cares what THEY make...it's OUR margin, and OUR cost/overhead structure that matters? So go compare pricing on a few key products...a C30, an F30 HB, a V30, and a J30...

Let's do easy math and assume their pricing is the same...you then know we currently make the same "X" bps on those products...so equal margin for this new location and they won't feel any pricing pain (assuming overhead is consistent also).

If their pricing is worse, you translate the pricing variance into bps and either make more on that location or give them some of it in rate, to help the transition... and gain more traction in the new market.

But if our pricing is worse, we may give up on/lose that deal or we just accept lower margins, or do some other cuts, etc., to gain a foothold in the new market.

Decisions, decisions... Lots of alternatives, but think smart, know your facts, know your numbers...

MOVE FORWARD!

Yours Truly,

Mr. Tenkey

#36

Dear Management,

So, I'm sitting here typing away in the den… and thinking, hmmm…this must be what it's like to work from home full-time. The sun shining, being totally focused, no interruptions, emails done, plans made… and FEELING GOOD!

Then reality sets in… The dog is barking to be let out…maybe I should rake up all the leaves, since it's so nice…oh, what did he just say on the TV playing in the background?…hmmm, I'm hungry…I'd better get this laundry caught up…Oops, wasn't I supposed to be on a phone call?

Now, now…settle down, all you telecommuters. I'm not against working from home. I HAVE pondered the idea.

But, let's get real…working from home is NOT ALWAYS a great thing ALL of the time.

So managers… DON'T give it away like candy.

And think it through. Ask yourself are this employee's duties team based/dependent or individual based/dependent? Is the employee self-directing? Is the employee productive alone? Are there cost savings? Can IT support the setup?

And remember, this is NOT a forever thing. Evaluate on a regular basis that it's working in terms of productivity and efficiency, for the business at hand.

Yours Truly,

Mr. Tenkey

#37

Dear Management,

What if you thought of the "employee on-boarding process" this way...

You're the parents, sitting in the living room, as your son or daughter opens the front door to introduce you to their new best friend.

Do you scare them off by asking for their car insurance and latest drug results, or do you sit them down for a nice chat and fresh cookies? Ohhhhhh, those first impressions...

Remember, you're in the service industry...your best asset is? (Hint: your employees). Your goal? That their first day is the BEST first day they've ever had.

So, ditch the old stack of paperwork, go digital, improve, update, SIMPLIFY, stop asking the "if you were a tree" questions, or ugh, those personality tests. I mean really...are you going to turn down a $50-million dollar producer because their aura is green and not blue?

Oh—and always have a STELLAR HR department, one that truly cares about the employee experience...change things up, make it fun.

How will you know if you're doing it right? The EMPLOYEE will show you...in every action they do from that point forward.

Yours Truly,

Mr. Tenkey

#38

Dear Management,

Efficiency is the NAME of the game. Every department, every system is under the microscope these days.

A couple of processing options for you:

- Centralized processing. Generally the strongest way to monitor usage, allocate availability, train new people, disseminate new processes, etc.

- Branch/LO processing. Generally the best way to support a top producer, get solid hands on sales support at the branch level, etc. In pure form, this is the sales "feel good" methodology.

But which is the best plan for cost and efficiency and more importantly, production enhancing? Can you tell which is which? Or my opinion?

It's centralized processing for all EXCEPT those LOs deemed worthy of us NEEDING to make them feel good.

Yours Truly,

Mr. Jenkey

#39

Dear Management,

Always be on lookout for efficiency anywhere and everywhere, even in the smallest process flows.

Why? Because I say so! But if that's not enough, think of it this way...

You have a 300-foot hallway down the center of your office, and you just found out Betty's kid was playing with Legos. He's no longer around, but he left 30 pieces here and there, up and down the length of it. (Did I mention they are the old-school SHARP jagged-edged ones?)

Now...your job is to get from one end of the hallway to the other, as FAST and efficiently as possible.

Oh wait, did I tell you about having to do this barefoot? And with the lights out?

OK: Get ready, get set, go!!! NOW tell me small items and obstructions in efficiency DON'T matter...

Yours Truly,

Mr. Tenkey

#40

Dear Management,

OK, let's play the "HIRE and FIRE" game!!!

You have two avatars to choose from...

- Avatar 1: The Educated Energizer Bunny (EEB). Powers include ability to make educated insightful decisions as opportunities avail themselves. Quick to find facts about the employee's referrals, skills assessment, productivity history...and hence, QUICK to hire. Also, quick to evaluate, assess, take corrective action...but knows when things go off track. So QUICK to fire as well (giving you extra leadership "respect coins" with other employees).

- Avatar 2: The Outdated Barca-lounging Grandpa (OBG). Powers include ability to make uneducated, un-insightful decisions as opportunities avail themselves. Slow to find facts about the employee's referrals, skills assessment, productivity history...and hence, as time goes on and on to gain consensus and/or data, SLOW to hire. Also, slow to evaluate, assess, or take corrective action when things go off track. So SLOW to fire as well. (Losing you extra leadership "respect coins" with other employees, who have to work beside the unproductive ones, who linger.)

Choose wisely, peeps!

And I leave you with this: "You down with EEB?" (Hint: Ya you know me.)

Yours Truly,

Mr. Jenkey

#41

Dear Management,

I was told once, "We don't care about the branch numbers, just tell us THE BOTTOM line."

I said, "OK...the company made $500,000 last month".

They told me, "Great. Let's move to the next subject."

I interrupted with, "BUT...if I may have a couple more moments."

I then went on to explain. "If we take a deeper look, branch 1 made us $5 million, branch 2 lost us $4 million, and branch 3 lost us $1/2 million. As you can see... things aren't really that GREAT. At first blush, we could have simply closed branches 2 and 3 and possibly saved that $4.5-million-dollar loss.

So DO you care about the branch numbers now?

Of course this example has been simplified, but you get the point. (And don't just default to the branch level, dig deeper...find all the income stream levels that matter.)

If you don't separate, quantify, or match proper income and expense streams you will never know if you are losing your version of ($4.5 million) dollars.

Yours Truly,

Mr. Tenkey

#42

Dear Management,

Do you have a system/database that details ALL the datapoints you need to make decisions about employees?

You should...

It should have all the normal name, rank, and serial number kinda stuff, as well as age and work status information for census data collecting and for renewals, physical locations and/or profit center numbers for proper rent and overhead allocations, as well as direct revenue/expense entry coding.

It should have all wage, commission, and bonus details for proper cost analysis.

It should have all hire, fire, and rehire dates for proper 401(k) vesting analysis.

It should have all benefit selections and offerings for proper cost analysis, as well as proper testing for correctness...

I could go on...but you get the point.

This database should be the ONE-STOP shop for ALL employee data points that are relevant for testing the correctness of payroll, analyzing proper revenue/expense entry coding, analyzing proper expense allocations, and any other analysis that may be useful from this data.

So, yep, it's MUCHO IMPORTANTE, peeps!

Yours Truly,

Mr. Tenkey

#43

Dear Management,

Speaking of allocations...there are companies out there that allocate ALL overhead costs to their branches by volume. (Hint: This is not correct.)

And there are some that spread pairoffs by total volume, including best efforts. (Hint: This is not correct.)

OK, I know I've lost some of you, but this is a BIG deal.

Proper allocations can be the difference between making a GOOD or BAD business decision.

I could list examples until the cows come home, but let's just go through the MUST HAVES of proper allocation.

Make sure the methodology of the allocation is based upon the CORE SOURCE of the item being allocated. Be it FTEs, units, volume, employee type, etc. But even more important than that, BE CONSISTENT!

Why???

Because even the best of allocations cannot always (due to cost/benefit constraints) be 100% allocated by the core source.

More often, it's like core source "adjacent"—but a consistent allocation setup will override any unforeseen bumps. So THINK and be CONSISTENT!

Yours Truly,

Mr. Tenkey

#44

Dear Management,

Do you "fully vet" new ideas with your department brass, BEFORE you start giving commands to the enlisted grades?

You should...

Otherwise you're just creating noise to the daily harmony...and muddling the waters of process flow.

How can that be? Because you can't know ALL the possible side effects of your ideas, better than the people that run the various tasks of the organization.

BUT let's say for a moment that you do... I would say that's just as bad, because your company will never outgrow the death grip you have on it. (Hint: Honey, let go of the bumper, the kid needs to get to college.)

A good company—a growth-oriented company—is built on a consistency of mind and thought (well-developed thoughts) of its leadership...and the efficiency of the processes it creates.

So, pre-heat those ovens to a FULL 350°F. Because nothing is worse to feed to your employees, than a half-baked idea.

Yours Truly,

Mr. Tenkey

#45

Dear Management,

Not all my tips can be sexy, but they can be informative.

Let's tackle the MIP (mortgage insurance premium) -"ish" payment process.

I've seen many process setups through the years, and I've found the following to be the most efficient and the most error proof.

Have all the MI -"ish" payments for FHA, VA, USDA and Reverse, etc. be paid by the funding department. They are closest to the loan and they are literally IN the loan at funding. They are also a good double check to rate calcs, missed credits, etc.

From there, accounting can take over and record the funding... match the funding receivable, with the investor ACH payment made. This is a good double-check against mismatched amounts, missed payments, etc.

"Lender paid" amounts require a couple of tweaks. Have funding initiate the request, accounting pay and record the payment, and then forward the data to shipping to be the double-check.

OK, we're done...the CEOs and Presidents can wake up now!

BUT be glad there are people in your company who are awake. Otherwise, you'd have UNSELLABLE LOANS.

Yah, I knew that'd keep you awake.

Yours Truly,

Mr. Tenkey

#46

Dear Management,

Aliens have just abducted you...they need help running a mortgage company back on their home planet of Ork.

You must be tested, though...but how?

They place you into a machine that scans your brain and builds a maze created from your leadership skills...that's how.

The test starts with your A-team being dropped into the middle of the maze... They must find their way out, using only the skills you have bestowed upon them as a leader.

Scared yet?

You shouldn't be...because you obviously have been consistent in your decisions, explained the whys of your decisions, and empowered and trained people to think without you needing to be there.

Do you think they make it out?

Now go ask someone not beholden to your ego and see if your answers match.

Leadership matters! Even on planet Ork...

Yours Truly,

Mr. Tenkey

#47

Dear Management,

Remember "One ringy dingy...two ringy dingy"—Lily Tomlin's phone operator skit?

Ugh, Google it, people... (Damn I'm old).

Well, anyway, here's my point. Just like the phone operator of old, technology swooped in and transformed all and now is forgotten. The same things are happening with loan process positions today. At a pace that hasn't been seen.

Change in our industry has moved slowly, focusing mainly on the loan operating systems, etc., but now the loan process duties themselves. The traditional processor role HAS been...that of the right arm to the loan officer...the organizer, the steady hand, the calmer of chaos.

But now, due to technology, chaos is being resolved by advanced CRMs and POSs...traditional tasks by pushes of button...and loan program analysis by AI.

The processors of old are having to step up, or unfortunately out. Their roles are merging with that of the traditional LOA type positions. So?

My point? Um...what are you doing?

Are you staying in step? Ahead? Evolving? Making sure these process changes are done in a way to gain on the efficiencies?

Keep up, people!

Yours Truly,

Mr. Tenkey

#48

Dear Management,

The new customers are different than those of yesterday. This is something banks have known for years...but for mortgage companies, it's LESSON time!

Banks have around been since the beginning...and as such their customer base has always been from babies to blue-hairs. Banks (fortunately) have always been capitalized well enough to cater to their changing customer base needs and technology advancements.

Take the integration of the ATM. They had to have a high-cost, brick-and-mortar, teller-intense, personal touch system in place for the blue hairs (who didn't trust machines to give them their money)...and cater to the babies who demanded nothing but the convenience of the ATM.

Mortgage companies have been able to drag their feet on changing the process. Getting a loan 60 years ago was pretty similar to 40 years, 15 years, or even 5 years ago (if you take out the "liar loan" days). BUT 5 years from now, that will not be the case.

Change is here, and the babies of today are demanding something DIFFERENT. So decisions have to be made big-time.

Does your company die with the blue hairs, reinvent itself for the babies, or straddle the hybrid line of serving both? Profits and staying in business are on the line.

Decide wisely...

Yours Truly,

Mr. Jenkey

#49

Dear Management,

You're in a boxing ring, gloves on...doing your best little bob and sway. The bell rings and here comes the opponent.

They wind up...you see it coming...a round-house alley-oop left hook.

What do you do? Turn to your corner and ask your team and all the participants in the front row for ideas? (Let me help you here: NOPE!)

Because, you've already had the strategic game plan meetings with your team to predict your opponent's moves...AND you have listened to their advice and you "Duck, stupid! Duck!" Then you do your super-duper uppercut and drop the competition to the floor.

The moral to this story?

Have a core group that meets regularly, hashes out options, sets the course. Listen to them, and plan out the fights (even the unplanned ones).

Train! Fight! Win! But if you have to kiss the mat a few times...

Learn! Retool! Fight again another day!

Yours Truly,

Mr. Tenkey

#50

Dear Management,

In an early tip, I noted the changes occurring with traditional processor tasks... due to advances in technology. But where else across the company are possible "technology" pickups?

Are you looking? You should...

RE-ASK yourself: How can I underwrite stronger...better? Are there junior underwriters who can push buttons and upload data, to speed things up? Can disclosures be done by the LO, with AI-assisted software? With LO volume levels lower these days...is turning in a clean file un-askable anymore? Can software help this process? Do you need to pay for LOAs, when a general admin person can push the same buttons for the whole branch combined? Can closing/funding/shipping tasks be redesigned through software for better process flow?

Leave no department unreviewed. Are marketing, secondary, accounting, and HR using the best tools available? AND is your IT dept up for the challenge, or is an external look needed?

A cautionary note, though. YES to review and innovation...BUT be mindful of capital limitations, grandfathered infrastructure limitations, and "change burnout" of the employees.

A ship whose course is corrected too abruptly, can end props up...

Yours Truly,

Mr. Jenkey

#51

Dear Management,

You've had a heck of a time with the product mix sitting at 15% bonds. You've rallied the troops, notified them why this product is killing the bottom line... you've looked at alternatives, started pushing niche tweaks to FHA products...

BUT did you see all this coming?

Can you tell if the trend is ending? Do you know if your effort to sway to more government loans is happening? Are you watching the product mix of your open pipeline, or for that matter the current month's fundings? Do you know the impact to the margins? Do you know if JUMBOs are back with a vengeance, or which of those are the good and bad?

For ALL of the above...you should!

Product mix is JUST as important as the volume numbers you praise so dearly...

Yours Truly,

Mr. Tenkey

#52

Dear Management,

How many of you predicted that Dennis Rodman would become a diplomatic superstar back in 2013, for his befriending of Kim Jong Un?

It's OK, I never saw that one coming either...

But now tell me how good you are at predicting what your volume will be in 7 months? If you tell me "I got this!"...then I bet you have a bridge in Brooklyn to sell me too, huh?

Trends only go so far, and history only tells so much...and only for a few months at best... The "estimated guess" factor goes sideways exponentially, beyond that point. Don't fret over finding a silver bullet...a 3-month window is fine for trend analysis.

Beyond that, always stay flexible enough to scale your overhead for any possible volume swing.

Stop trying to be a Fortune Teller. Be a Boy Scout instead...and just be PREPARED.

Because "I PREDICT" is the best answer.

Yours Truly,

Mr. Jenkey

#53

Dear Management,

Are you doing proper forest management? Or will you be the sawmill that gets mothballed?

Even the mightiest of high-volume cedars has a harvest date...so not only do you have to worry about your top producers getting shopped, you have to worry about their expiration...

Have you planned for that? Have you planted new seedlings this year? Last year? The year before that? Have you rooted out any bad infestations? Have you watered and fertilized the growing saplings?

Can we all say it together? "You should!!!!"

So unless you want your company to retire along with your top producers...

PLANT for the future harvest!

Yours Truly,

Mr. Tenkey

#54

Dear Management,

Seems like LOs are being shopped more diligently than ever before...but it might just seem that way, due to the depths into the "limited volume" bucket some companies are going...and fighting so mercilessly for.

Why?

I'm not sure it's the best move, but some companies think the cost of buying the market or bringing pain to the competition...is worth their own pained bottom line. I hope they're running the long-term effects of (at least) breaking even on these moves.

I often think they aren't when I hear the numbers being paid for an LO doing one or two loans a month. I often think it's a blessing in disguise for the company being pilfered...it eliminates a low-producing, overhead-eating LO and often triggers that company to rethink the tried and true 80/20 rule, and where their "LO retention" efforts should be focused.

So the moral is...

If you're one of those companies doing the pilfering...think wisely of your tactics and their costs.

And if you're one of the companies being pilfered...think of the blessing in disguise...of the "re-focus" on WHY an LO would stay, or SHOULD have been let go, and you hesitated.

Yours Truly,

Mr. Jenkey

#55

Dear Management,

And speaking of LO retention tools...

Guess who's back... Back again. Phantom's back. Tell a friend. Guess who's back? Guess who's back? Guess who's back?

Yes...that deferred comp perennial itself...phantom stock is back! But is it a "silver bullet"?

Now, these things can be great. They pass income to pinpointed producers without fear of LO comp rules, they can delay the timing of payments in a way to retain (golden handcuff) key players (nonproducing as well), they are totally flexible in setup, and they DO NOT give up/play around with voting rights or shares/stocks.

They can also be a Pandora's Box that the key players end up ignoring or resenting, as well as an administrative nightmare.

SO, keep these things simple!

Think of it this way...whatever setup you come up with, it needs to be able to be fully conveyed and absorbed in a 2-minute elevator ride.

Yours Truly,

Mr. Tenkey

#56

Dear Management,

Underwriters are being attacked by technology (specifically due to AI), more than even a coal miner these days... Are you positioning your company for the aftermath?

You should!

Rethink old tactics of placing junior underwriters to train up and take over lesser tasks you don't want in high dollar U/W hands...because there may not be U/W jobs available to train them into...and with the advancements in AI, there may not be "lesser tasks" for them, either.

Underwriting, faster than most departments...is being redesigned daily.

How this will end? It's still being written...

This much is known: U/Ws are going to have a different position in the future. They will be even higher skilled and much more focused on big-picture risk (things "AI" can't evaluate, for now).

AND companies will have fewer of them.

So to companies: Stay in tune with advancements BUT don't be the beta site, if you can't afford it. Just be ready to pounce on efficiency when you can.

Also, be ready to make hard decisions of who goes and who stays, when those decisions are necessary. The U/W role is going to be more important and more refined in coming years.

And to U/Ws: What can I say? Train up and prove your worth, your world is changing fast.

Yours Truly,

Mr. Jenkey

#57

Dear Management,

Have you thought about a "what if" for losing a key player?

What is your plan B? Do you even have one? You should...

Be it a producer, or an ops person, or an exec. Life can throw you a lot of curve balls. Are you ready to swing and hit that sweet spot, when it does?

Your company can rebound much faster and with far less grief, if you are.

Yours Truly,

Mr. Tenkey

#58

Dear Management,

Along with good forest maintenance, comes using the right tools...so let's take CRMs for a moment.

They are expensive, time consuming to set up, and more to maintain. BUT they are "proven" and they do work.

They help maintain connection and order to your borrower base. That's a GOOD thing.

The hard part is, if you are new to the game, then you have an established forest that has done well for you...without using a CRM and will be hard pressed to be proven that they are doing things wrong and should try this. So buy-in will be slow and focused on the next generation.

Just hope you have the patience and dollars to ride the time-line out. And who knows, maybe the established stock will see the pickup the youngsters are getting and dabble in themselves.

So know your user, and spend accordingly for the expected ROI.

Yours Truly,

Mr. Jenkey

#59

Dear Management,

Are you losing LOs to "Broker-dom"? You know...the land where everything is GOLD, where they are the boss, where they make all the decisions, where they get all the money, where they get all the best pricing, blah blah blah...

Market conditions are prime for this, and there are some great TPO (third party origination) arrangements out there... where a seasoned LO, with a good production pool AND a good business sense, can clean up.

Problem is, most LOs (like most people) are not hard-wired to be good at both sales and operations. BUT THAT won't be in their head when they leave you for the end of the rainbow that some wholesalers are pointing out to them.

What can you do? You can make your company the best it can be...AND educate your LOs about what is involved on the back side of decision making and costs of running a business. (Show your worth.)

BUT if that doesn't work, join them (maybe)? And no, not to become a broker. But maybe open a TPO channel? You already have the infrastructure. Just needs tweaking and hey, you get to offload a lot of costly expenses.

I mean if you're gonna keep the risk, why not a reward, too? There are pitfalls, but with a good team behind you, it is a VERY viable game plan. OPTIONS, people!

Yours Truly,

Mr. Tenkey

#60

Dear Management,

Every department in your organization has a defined place and purpose.

Take these three...

Secondary sets the street price that makes sure your company is competitive, while capturing a much-needed MARGIN level.

Underwriting sets your risk tolerance, hence mitigating losses that could eat up that MARGIN.

Accounting sets the efficiency marks, and creates the analytics to crystal ball what is happening with that MARGIN.

Yes, these three...they make sure all the efforts of getting all those loans in the door, produce MARGIN (aka PROFIT).

Choose wisely who leads these departments. It can have a DRAMATIC effect on not only those specific departments' setup, but more importantly your bottom line.

CHOOSE wisely, peeps!

Yours Truly,

Mr. Jenkey

#61

Dear Management,

This tip is a tribute to my Dad.

So the word here is "ingenuity." The kind of ingenuity that takes duct tape and a pair of pliers and gets the car running again...and saves the family vacation. The kind of ingenuity that mixes left-over paint cans together to come up the perfect "original" color to paint the inside of the garage...

So in that vein, are you smaller lenders (really this is to all of you) keeping track of profitability at the loan level "within" your accounting systems?

No? Why not?

If my Dad could do what he did, you can take the job-costing module of your system (at a minimum) and tie the job number/loan number and track away! All the income and expenses that can be tagged to jobs/loans through your receipts, a/p, journal entries, and so on.

And FYI, I've done this with QuickBooks—so really, there are no excuses out there.

And with that, you can thank my Dad.

Yours Truly,

Mr. Tenkey

#62

Dear Management,

Are Non-QM (qualified mortgage) loans the gateway drug to Sub Prime?

Me? Well, I think they can be...

The collective memory of the world is short these days, the margin compression is giving all companies a reason to pause, housing prices are limiting buyers from getting in or moving up...all PRIME conditions to look for a silver bullet in the open arms of the repackaged savior...NON-QMs.

And when you look back, Option ARMs (adjustable rate mortgage) were NOT an evil beast...they were great financial vehicles for the RIGHT borrowers. It was the people (always the people...) who used them for greed and threw little 'ole caution to the wind...

So be cautious, peeps! Follow good business decisions...not the almighty dollar, and all will be good.

Yours Truly,

Mr. Jenkey

#63

Dear Management,

As a leader, a misstep happens...

Are you a resolute-er or a persecute-er?

Your answer sets the tone of your company...from being open, creative, free-flowing...to being closed, stifling, uninventive.

Resolute-er = leadership that looks at missteps from an enterprise view. Looking at where the process went wrong...why did it happen? Where did a thought process go wrong? And so on.

Employees feel they are part of the solution...as it's used as a learning tool...a "Where we can get better?" tool, or if needed, a "Someone is in the wrong position" evaluator. The main goal is to fix the process/procedure, learn from it, and fight another day.

Persecute-er = leadership that looks at missteps as a court case that needs to be solved.

Employees are turned into suspects and witnesses (against one another). The focus is not where did the process fail, but WHO failed. False arrests happen...people get left in positions they shouldn't be left in. Employees feel their main goal is to NOT make another mistake. It STIFLES their creativity, for fear of possible future failure. The main goal is to win the case...not resolve the underlying issue. So, don't be a persecute-er!

Now you know...and knowing is half the battle.

Yours Truly

Mr. Tenkey

#64

Dear Management,

Do you know how to calculate the monthly volume every LO must fund to keep the doors open?

And not only the doors open, but themselves employed? (And no, that's not harsh...they get paid premium pay for a reason, and they should earn it.)

So again, do you? You should...

And there are a lot of methods to get there, but in some fashion you need to sum your fixed expense components and divide them by how many LOs you have. That result is then divided by your variable margin...

And voila! Your monthly volume each LO must obtain, in order to earn their keep.

And remember to factor in those things that this simple formula won't, like paying extra to LOs for assistants, pricing exceptions, marketing, etc... That will help with weighting the results.

Happy discovering, peeps!

Yours Truly,

Mr. Tenkey

#65

Dear Management,

Let's clarify why proper usage of allocations is VERY critical to interpreting a correct story from the financials.

Take three branches for 1 month:

Branch #1 (5 FHAs) (Vol $1,250,000)
Branch #2 (1 JUMBO) (Vol $1,000,000)
Branch #3 (4 HELOCs) (Vol $100,000)

Now I'm going to allocate one overhead item, Corporate U/W, down to the branch level.

The worst interpretation would be simple allocation by volume. Think of it this way—does it take more U/W time for 1 JUMBO then 5 FHA loans? The answer is no, so why penalize #2 and make it look less efficient?

A satisfactory interpretation would be allocation by units. This is OK, if done consistently, and adjusting for Broker and seconds on a weighted percentage. Remember the old standby, volume drives profit...units drive costs.

The best thing would be to do actual job costing of labor per (specific) loan and allocate the nonspecific items by those results. Yeppers!

So...

Work with your specific system limitations, BUT strive for better...and once you land on a methodology... be consistent!

Misinterpreted financials become MISSED opportunities.

Yours Truly,

Mr. Tenkey

#66

Dear Management,

Did you know...that NOT knowing all the answers is...OK?

Yep...

In the "How to be a good leader handbook" (oh, you know somebody's written it), it states that leadership is not based on how much you know, but rather by how much you build.

So build a great team around you...one that fills in where you lack—yes, lack, no one is perfect, even you...

You're the idea, the spark, the risk-taker. Build a team that makes you bigger than you think you are.

But don't forget that you NEED them and they NEED you... (Hint: Teamwork makes the dream work.)

So go build something GREAT!

Yours Truly,

Mr. Tenkey

#67

Dear Management,

I celebrated the life of my Dad...of course the tears, but so many more smiles, as I talked with all the well-wishers throughout the celebration.

So even though sadness, let's make this a learning moment...

It got me thinking about your companies. What if you were to lose a high-impact voice? And losing them through whatever form they may leave...

Are you positioning for that as a possibility? Do you know who those pivot people are? Are you mentoring others to be able to step into those possible voids?

You should...

Let those lost voices and what they brought to the table carry on...even though they may walk down different paths...

Because I can tell you...even though Dad is no longer with us, I will forever do home projects...based on the foundation of workmanship he taught me.

#neverforgotten

Yours Truly,

Mr. Tenkey

#68

Dear Management,

So you have a scorecard (or at least you should) that gives you the production characteristics of each LO, for some set time period...

Well, whoopie...what about the profitability characteristics of each LO? I like to NOT infer who is the most productive, I like to prove it.

Example:
LO #1, four conventional loans a month.
LO #2, four FHA loans a month.

If you stop at prod-level details only, LO #2 wins every day. FHA loans bring in more margin.

If you add profitability characteristics...you'll bring in things like how many assistants, spacing requirements, pricing exceptions, tolerance cures, comm structure, headache factor, etc.

With all this info I discover that for LO #2 we pay for two assistants, 50 more bps per loan, their own satellite office, and a $5k monthly marketing allowance... (exaggerated of course).

But you get the point. As much as LO #1 looks like the top pick every day...

Think, peeps...use the right data points and the truth is always revealed...

Yours Truly,

Mr. Tenkey

#69

Dear Management,

I've learned a lot about cancer lately...about the way it works within your body, sometimes completely hidden...sometimes just acute aches and pains.

Much like companies with "those" employees (from receptionists to executives) who work within your organization, causing pain and turmoil to the natural order.

But there is always a day of reckoning...when the balance of symptoms requires a visit to the doctor.

But WHY wait sooooooooo long?

Think of teachers in the staff lounge...every one of them knows who the bad pills of the school are. You should, too...

So...radiate them or remove them (continuing the cancer analogy).

The alternative? The WHOLE system becomes "those" employees, because the "others" assimilate or leave.

Yours Truly,

Mr. Tenkey

#70

Dear Management,

Are you marketing like it's *Nine-teen, Nine-tay... Nine*? Or, do *Doves Cry* when they look at your outdated flyers?

Repeat after me, "Flyers are DEAD and drip email campaigns are as ANNOYING as they sound."

So, what to do?

DIFFERENTIATE yourself!

STAND OUT! BE CREATIVE!

Pick your niche...Who's your audience? Where do they hang out online? Do you have a flagpole waving there for them to see?

Be it social media, videos, blogs, etc., are you using today's tools to build your network? To offer help? To share advice? To MAKE A PRESENCE in other peoples' lives?

You should...

Yours Truly,

Mr. Jenkey

#71

Dear Management,

Based on new information...are you open to altering your opinions?

You should be...

But not everything new and shiny is good...so your opinion doesn't HAVE to change.

How about, before you go off in search of new information, working with what you have to make it the best you can...WITH what you have.

THEN, or even better during that time, take new opinions in to make an even BETTER outcome.

Too often, people search for the next shiny penny—that "silver bullet"—only to end up with a BIG stack of pennies and a trail of wasted efforts.

Yours Truly,

Mr. Tenkey

#72

Dear Management,

Are you tired of looking at 5-year projections, scattered over multiple spreadsheets...all to decide if a prospective branch is worthy of a "yes" vote?

Me too...

Financial analysis can be FUN...(YES it can!) and for you doubters...it can be CONCISE as well.

There is NO reason for more than one page PER profit center. I will allow a summary page ONLY if there are multiple profit centers.

And I'm not talking about leaving stuff off to make it fit. I'm saying make the items on the page MORE meaningful...lump assumptions into bps instead of line iteming the little things. LESS data points, MORE impact!

And what's up with the 5-year projections? Anybody who could have told me what the mortgage industry would have done in 2018 would have just thrown a lucky dart...

Make the analysis tell you a story.

And WHAT story?

Whether you give a thumbs up or down on a new a profit center(s)...

The End

Yours Truly,

Mr. Tenkey

#73

Dear Management,

What should you do with the excess cash you have lying around???

First, before you go spending...determine what is "lying around." Because a natural dilemma of service organizations are net worth req's with no real assets to speak of (other than cash).

So take the gross cash figure and subtract covenant req's, investor delegation req's, operational and payroll rolling req's, rainy day fund req's, etc.

So how much is left? THAT is your play money.

You can use it for such things as offsetting cost of funds, growth initiatives, bonus for a fabulous CFO, buying a company limo, etc.

And DON'T FORGET to manage those cash needs (and the changes in them) through your daily cash standing report.

You don't have one?

You should...

Yours Truly,

Mr. Tenkey

#74

Dear Management,

BE (breakeven) analysis is great and all, but have you ever tried WAIDT (why am I doing this) analysis?

Don't know what that is? You should...

Conventional BE analysis focuses on what volume level covers all your costs, so you don't lose a dollar...but unfortunately, it also keeps that $0 dollar balance in your bank account.

While WAIDT analysis focuses on what volume is needed to make all this worthwhile: ownership and employees earning a satisfying pay, all growth and efficiency goals met, employees are productive and positive, production systems humming, loan officers happy, etc.

THAT number is WAY more important than a simple BE calculation.

One gives you the WHAT volume is needed and the WHY you're trying to get there. The other just tells you how to stay where you are...

#moveforwardpeople

Yours Truly,

Mr. Tenkey

#75

Dear Management,

Rising house prices and low inventory were bound to result in this. With newfound equity and no way to spend it...all hail the return of the standalone second and HELOCs as viable products once again.

And with that, investors are raising margins (Yeah!). But they are also telling everyone, including LOs (Boo!).

And like every other human...when LOs smell more pie, they start asking for their piece.

Easy fix? Well before all the LO comp rules (remember the good 'ole days?), I would have said yes. Now creativity is the new normal in pay structures. And the CFPB is NO help on clarity.

So you already have a plan in place...probably not paying or including either of these products in pay calcs...what do you do now?

Grid out your current pay structures, isolate these two products. Create new, but don't give away the bank. And yes...it can be done, but the comp rules DON'T make it easy.

Just like what happened with low-margin JUMBOs, creativity brought us commission caps.

Gotta love regulators who write the rules, but don't understand how to operationally put them in place.

But hey, it keeps us bean counters employed, right? Ugh...

Yours Truly,

Mr. Tenkey

#76

Dear Management,

Does your company...or do your loan officers...have:

A dynamic website? A Facebook page? A LinkedIn page? A Blog? A Podcast? An Instagram page?

Do you create online ads/marketing...that drives business to them?

Do you know what SEO stands for?

You should...

And if you are/do...that's great, but are you/they building content that CREATES A PRESENCE? That drives a borrower to do nothing else but make (whatever the online version is these days) the phone ring?

If not...you're just a parent, trying to be "with it" in front of your kid's friends...

Yours Truly,

Mr. Jenkey

#77

Dear Management,

OK, can we just admit that "net" (oops, can't say that)...I mean "creatively compensated" branches DO exist?

And they aren't special...they're just a defined compensation arrangement for bringing production/branches/etc. to the table.

So call it...name it...describe it...market it...what you will...but guess what? Still not special...

Let me demonstrate:

Each of the following branches produces four identical apple pies...four pieces each.

Branch 1 is an Enterprise Branch. The branch manager gets one piece per pie.

Branch 2 is the Manager's Pot of Gold Branch. The branch manager gets none of the first three pies, but gets 100% of the fourth pie.

Branch 3 is the NOTTA Net Branch. For each each pie, the branch manager gets 1/2 of 50% of the total crust and 100% of the filling, but is charged a 75% filling fee.

Which one would you choose? (Hint: They all end up the same.)

Think PIE people...DON'T over-complicate it...just DIVIDE it and move on...

So much time is being eaten up creating a nightmare of administration...to end up no different than a simple % split at the end of the day.

#stoptheinsanity

Yours Truly,

Mr. Tenkey

#78

Dear Management,

So, you're packing up the car for a wonderful weekend of woods, campfires, and s'mores...

Only to have your MORE significant other tell you they've decided you're now going to the beach.

So now you unpack, repack, and set off on a great weekend at the beach...No shoes, no shirts, no problems...

Only to find out your MORE significant other, is no longer feeling "it" and just wants to stay home.

UGH!!!! Right?

But guess what? You just may be that "MORE significant other" to your employees...

So STOP changing your mind!

Here's what it does. It makes your employees insane at first, and then they start doing the least amount of work to show they're making progress, but assuming a change is coming. It's TOTALLY inefficient. It shows a lack of thinking through the entire process up front.

And yes, changes do happen that you can't foresee...BUT that happens with the experience of actually implementing a plan and testing results along the way...

So if that has not happened, YOU ARE that "MORE significant other"!

Yours Truly,

Mr. Jenkey

#79

Dear Management,

If you were a superhero and I was the Alfred to your Batman (Hint: The loyal sidekick)...

I would tell you this...

Words matter!

Action (by example) of those words is your yellow sun.

Hypocrisy of those words is your kryptonite!

Yours Truly,

Mr. Tenkey

#80

Dear Management,

Want to know one of the biggest ways to increase both efficiency AND the bottom line?

I figured you'd continue reading after that one...so let's get to it.

Everyone always relates a company's efficiency to its operations...how to process faster, underwrite faster, close faster, streamline this, streamline that.

But what about Sales? Why is Sales so often left off the table when it comes to this realm?

Why not think about what happens along the path from first chat to triggering a loan? Who is closing the deals? Why are they better? Why are we losing the other deals? Can technology help?

Do we need to train better? Is our pricing out of touch? Do our loan officers even know the inefficiency they're pushing down the track?

Other "costly" things to look at...How much is spent on marketing and advertising? Which marketing campaigns are making an impact? Which are not? If paying for leads, is it worth it?

Is our office space and other associated costs appropriate? Should we centralize office admin/processing costs?

Find these answers and you win...the pot of gold that shows up on your bottom line!

Yours Truly,

Mr. Jenkey

#81

Dear Management,

Do you think the President of (name your favorite fast food chain) JUST HAS TO KNOW if an employee making a double burger in Longview, Washington is wearing the appropriate work shoes?

I'll answer for you. NO, they do not.

They have discovered that letting go...LET'S YOU GROW!

And who did they let go to...? A competent management team that transformed their sketch of an idea...into reality.

Barring following that path...DO NOT complain to me about: being sooooooo overworked, all the fires you wish others would take care of, or NOT being able to grow to the true potential of your vision.

Remember that $5 mirror I told you about in prior tips? Use it!

Yours Truly,

Mr. Tenkey

#82

Dear Management,

Use AMCs or start an In-House Appraisal Division? Which to choose, which to choose...?

AMCs

Pros
Many and various AMCs to choose from
Easy cancellation for poor performance
Less concern about the appearance of non-independence of the appraisers

Cons
The AMCs have other customers, with needs as important as yours
Bound to the turn times they are able to provide
The work output could be fraught with negligent appraisals, and a lack of accountability also

In-House Appraisal Division

Pros
The highest level of control over service performance
Procedures and performance levels can be tailor-made to your company's requirements
All the division's employees and appraisers are focused on providing the best service to your company

Cons
Must beef up procedures to cancel any appearance of non-independence of the appraisers
More difficult to unwind if it does not work out as planned
Hidden costs for overhead burden for minimum level requirements...exacerbated by "non-buy-in" of LOs to the In-House process

So choose wisely...from which pros and cons you can live with.

Yours Truly,

Mr. Jenkey

#83

Dear Management,

The mortgage industry is a roller coaster of alternating profitable and no-so-profitable times. Always has been, always will be.

In those times, when you rally the troops to cut pay, cut hours, cut bonuses, cut fellow employees, cut, cut, cut...while asking those same people to hold the tide, dig deep, cover the duties of fallen comrades, etc., etc., etc...

Do you remember those things? That they did what you asked of them? That they helped you ride that storm?

Then as fast as you cut, you should be just as quick in repairing those sacrifices.

You may have forgotten and moved on to the next wave, but those soaked by the crash of the last wave did not...

Yours Truly,

Mr. Tenkey

#84

Dear Management,

Guess what? I'm YOUR customer...and I DON'T want to fill out your damn survey!

Ok, maybe that's a little harsh, but it's a pet peeve. And what happened to providing good customer service? End of story.

Isn't it enough that I used your service/product, spent my good money, and shook your hand after a good job was done?

Because it seems these days, I can't even use a company's restroom without getting a survey sent to see if I enjoyed the experience.

Why do I now have to rehash the experience by either lying and overstating the experience to make you feel better (not me, THE CUSTOMER) or understating the experience and getting nothing taken care of but maybe a phone call to rehash my bad experience (which, guess what...now I'm gonna tell more friends, because I am more annoyed).

My preference: If I like you, I refer your service/product; and if I don't, I consider it a lesson learned and speak with my dollars and non-referral.

But maybe that's just me...thanks for letting me rant.

Yours Truly,

Mr. Tenkey

#85

Dear Management,

"Game of Thrones" may be settled...but what about the hierarchy of your organization?

Are the right people rising up the noble ranks? Are they honorable? Are they great leaders?

Or have they schemed to destroy the kingdoms of their fellow lords and ladies? Do they have ill regard for the common people?

Be careful of the people you surround yourself with...think more Sansa Stark and less Cersei Lannister when you're selecting your round table (yes, I know that's King Arthur, but you get my point).

Yours Truly,

Mr. Tenkey

#86

Dear Management,

How do you relay information on products, scenarios, procedures, etc. to your sales force?

For us in operations, policies and procedures, and the training of those said items, are our map to success.

What is happening on your sales side? And yes, sales can do other things than "I need them out there getting more loans." So with that, can we all agree to stop using that tired excuse?

Learning about new products, how to sell them, new market strategies AND new procedures (yes, procedures) to get loans through the system faster is NOT a bad thing...

Sales is not operations (I get it), but structure for the unstructured is a balancing act that a good sales leadership team MUST master.

Think of it this way...when you pull up to the gas pump in your 1969 Camaro... do you just buy regular or choose the premium high octane your classic beauty deserves?

Feed that engine properly!

Yours Truly,

Mr. Jenkey

#87

Dear Management,

How many minutes does it take to hard boil an egg?

Answer: My Grandma says 8 minutes.

So why, then, are you testing eggs at 2, 3.5, 4, and 6 minutes? It's an egg...you hired a great chef...STOP breaking open half-cooked eggs!

INSTEAD: Set an expectation, define the task, wait until the task is complete, and THEN turn into the food critic.

If you're happy, yeah! If you're unhappy, make it a learning lesson. Or if the lesson can't be learned...it's new chef time.

Think of all that unproductive time you're spending now, that can be focused on things that actually move the company forward...

Bon Appetit!

Yours Truly,

Mr. Tenkey

#88

Dear Management,

Are you keeping up on trends? I'm not talking about outside the company (although those are important, but just not for this tip). I'm talking more about the internal ones, the ones that drive your company.

You should be...

Even when times are good...keep an eye toward the horizon and better efficiency. So often in our industry, funding improves, people get busier, and trends/waste get overlooked.

Ugh, people! Our industry is a wave machine...be diligent with trending. Don't be caught by the next one crashing down on you...be ahead of it.

And why leave money on the table? The best time to make more money is when it's in your hands and plentiful. Hold on to more of it by being smart in the "hang ten" moments as well.

Now go check in with your financial analyst and thank them for their hard work.

Yours Truly,

Mr. Jenkey

#89

Dear Management,

Even though I just pushed internal trends, some equal time on external trends also...

Myopic views are not a great vantage point for healthy leadership. They can lead one to having an autocratic ruling hand.

Your company is NOT that unique, and the more you look inward for answers, the more you'll lose touch with industry-proven norms that have already passed the smell test...

Look outward, join peer groups, visit trade shows, conferences, etc.

I also find warehouse reps, MI reps, LinkedIn connections, etc., a great source for front-line intel...

Keep an eye outward too, peeps!

Yours Truly,

Mr. Tenkey

#90

Dear Management,

Should you buy a Fitbit or a rubber band?

But wait...first, what is your actual goal? Let's say for this tip, it's weight loss...

Here's why I bring this up. Depending on your goal, budget, infrastructure, etc., the next new-fangled gadget is NOT always the best option.

Fitbit: Cost $149.99, charging required, app updates required. Use: learn it, download apps, dock it, upload it, track things, know how many steps you did, blah, blah, blah... Lose weight.

Rubber band: Cost $0.01, no charging required, no maintenance needed. Use: put on wrist. When tempted by bad food, turn wrist to inner side, pull band, let go...distracted by pain and no longer tempted... Lose weight.

So based on your goal, why not choose the rubber band...which does the task, is 15,000 times less expensive, requires no charging or maintenance, will outlast the other option, AND if you choose a colored version, will match your outfit?

Yes, a funny comparison, but hopefully you get my point.

Choose the option that meets the goal, and don't chase the objects that are new and shiny, SIMPLY BECAUSE they are new and shiny.

Think through things, peeps!

Yours Truly,

Mr. Jenkey

#91

Dear Management,

It IS OK to just fade into the sunset with your company...that IS a viable business plan.

You're the owner, and if the current changes in the wind are not something you agree with or have it within you to change with...it is OK to plan for that.

I've said earlier that, up until now...change has come slow to the mortgage industry. The way we do loans is pretty similar to the way it was done 30 years ago. Yes, technology HAS moved in...BUT the process flow from app to funding, has remained pretty consistent.

And this move has been mostly driven by efficiency and from the demand of the companies.

But now, the borrowers are demanding change and technology is answering back big time and many companies just aren't ready...and MORE importantly, the Loan Officers aren't either.

Lots of ole' dogs in this industry...set in their ways...

So decide now...stop fighting and slip away quietly into that good night...or get ready to make some big decisions (and changes) and be uncomfortable in your skin for a while, until the industry finds a new normal.

Choose wisely.

Yours Truly,

Mr. Tenkey

#92

Dear Management,

Still holding onto that servicing pool?

You know...the one you set up when everyone thought the correspondent channel was ending?

Well, what are you doing with it now? Is your goal of a separate income stream being met?

No?

Then why keep it? If you're just keeping it to maintain your FNMA approval... have you heard of co-issue? Research it.

If you're not thinking of it as an income stream...maintaining it...feeding it with volume...

Sell it!

You're probably not getting the ROI you think you are anyway. But YOU ARE having the hassle of administration and licensing...and holding onto servicing liability.

The big lenders have the luxury of economies of scale to feed this income stream.

So if it's not working for your company, go talk to secondary and see what bids for the servicing pool can be had.

Good luck!

Yours Truly,

Mr. Jenkey

#93

Dear Management,

ALL employees need a pat on the back.

So, search for the "pat" that motivates them the best...

And what kinds of "pats" are there?

Well, duh...number one is money (no one is gonna work for you for free, or for less than the competition).

But just as important are things like acknowledgment, leadership opportunities, paths to advancement, skill building, working from home, additional vacation, and so on.

The real trick is to find out what "pat" to use...because some employees won't ask for that special "pat", they'll just leave...and leave you wondering...

Happy searching, peeps!

Yours Truly,

Mr. Tenkey

#94

Dear Management,

There are certain tasks that you hire for and certain that you don't? Do you know the difference?

You should...

Because certain tasks are best managed through contracts, not employment.

 For example:

Web design, for mid-sized lender, no internal knowledge base—CONTRACT.

Processing capacity, with robust internal processing staff and supervision, need extra capacity for bulge production—CONTRACT.

Marketing, for large lender, want to build a custom digital experience, well capitalized—HIRE.

Analytics, for small lender, no internal knowledge base—CONTRACT (at first).

Compliance, for mid-sized lender, to get a hold on risk AND process— HIRE.

See my point?

Focus on the task at hand, supervision, knowledge base, and of course the capitalization you have "in house." THEN choose accordingly.

Otherwise, come see me in a year when you're feeling my point first-hand.

Yours Truly,

Mr. Jenkey

#95

Dear Management,

I've heard this one a lot...

"We need to cut back on office overhead. Why do we need so many people? What are all these people doing?"

My response: You are the "deciders"...you make the choices that make the systems complex or NOT.

You're the ones that say it's OK to having 50 different pay structures and pay periods.

You're the ones who "do not" say no to carrying EVERY product type and going into EVERY state where a loan officer wants to vacation.

You're the ones who continue to bounce off the "deep gray" of compliance...causing the need for safety nets to be maintained.

You're the ones that lean too heavily toward sales, instead of a balance with best practices.

Etc., etc., etc.

MANAGEMENT creates the difficulty level of the company...the back office just answers the call.

If you want change...a smaller back office...then start everything with a KISS (keep it simple, stupid).

Yours Truly,

Mr. Tenkey

#96

Dear Management,

Can you ever get away from work? Do you constantly have to check in? Monitor things?

Then I say you should evaluate two things...

1. Let's start with the one that won't get you mad at me...You need to honestly evaluate the competency of your "next in command" employees. A few days or a few weeks with you gone should not bring a grinding halt to the company. If it does, then obviously they aren't up to the task.

2. If that's not it (and in most cases it isn't), then you need to honestly evaluate your training ability and whether you're not letting go enough...of the duties and authority necessary for them to succeed.

In the words of Elsa, "Let it go."

The BEST leaders are the ones that have built a team that can stand without them.

Now go lead... then leave...for a vacation!

Yours Truly,

Mr. Tenkey

#97

Dear Management,

Again...MAKE a decision!

ANY decision, SOME decision, even a BAD decision...

A decision provides a focus, a map, a guiding star. Even a bad decision provides a learning opportunity.

INDECISION provides LOSS...loss of everything...and most of all, loss of respect.

Yours Truly,

Mr. Tenkey

#98

Dear Management,

Do you know if your CFO is providing value?

You should...

Do they have a full vision of the company...beyond accounting?

Do you understand when they explain new concepts? Are these new concepts something they brought to the table? Do they go over your head with analysis and fancy words?

Are they a true business partner in your growth and prosperity?

Wrong answers above? NOT good...

A good CFO should be able to explain ANY business concept...to anyone from the front-line person, to the exec team.

So besides financial acumen, integrity, and the ability to communicate effectively... they need to be confident, convincing...and have foresight.

They must understand the FULL range and cycles of ALL aspects of the sales and operational sides of the company...and possess the leadership skills to command a following from all levels of that company.

They must understand the financial and MORE IMPORTANTLY the non-financial triggers that make all the "cogs in the wheel" move things forward.

It's the steps beyond the numbers, to process...to system flows...to external impacts...to human insights...that truly define a good CFO.

So, with all that, did you choose wisely? Yes? Yeah! No? Upgrade time!

Yours Truly,

Mr. Jenkey

#99

Dear Management,

Why is your starting point always to look outward for fixes/ideas? Did you know that often, the answers are already within the walls of your own company?

You should...

But maybe that's what you needed...to hear it from me...so you'll look back behind you...and remember back to all those things various employees have been telling you all along.

Maybe this time you'll listen with an open mind...

To all the fixes that they've proposed and you dismissed...
To the warnings that weren't heeded...
To the enthusiasm they've shut off because you ignored them...
To the times they tried, and now have given up...

The wake of a leader can provide a great surfing experience or flood the beach...

Your call.

Yours Truly,

Mr. Tenkey

#100

Dear Management,

Never push a loyal employee to the point where they no longer care…

Because these, these are the good ones…

The ones you need to care…the ones who may find somewhere else to care…

The ones who may…just write a book.

Yours Truly,

Mr. Jenkey

Thank you for listening…

Yours Truly,

Mr. Tenkey

THE END